CALIFORNIA BEAT POETRY

Volume One

-- Hollywood Boulevard --

John K Bucher

Sideshow Media Group
8033 Sunset Blvd. #164
Hollywood, CA. 90046

info@sideshowmediagroup.com

Published in Los Angeles, California, by Sideshow Media Group

Bulk copies of this book can be ordered by contacting:

Sideshow Media Group
8033 Sunset Blvd. #164
Hollywood, CA. 90046
info@sideshowmediagroup.com

Sideshow Small Books are inspired by *The Pocket Poetry Series* that **City Lights Bookstore** in San Francisco released to reinforce the work of Beat Poets.

They are designed to:

A) Fit into someone's back pocket so that they can be used in emergency situations

B) Be left in locations that are in need of poetry

Beat : beat down, beatnik, music beat, beat poets, Kerouac, Ginsberg.

This book is dedicated to anyone

who has ever been in love

or broke.

Seeing Ghosts

Late at night upon leaving the bar

A blue fendered Cadillac bearing
stars and starlets break out of the fog

The boulevard is back in time

I'm seeing ghosts, Bogart, Bacall,
Fields and Arbuckle, Chaplin,   Nichol-
son

They are all here, alive, dead, why does it
matter?

Hollywood and Highland,   Grau-
man's and El Captitan, Oscar walks the
street

The lights, the air, stolen moments,
dreams

Rest on the palmy street with the
ghosts' names on the sidewalks

The boulevard has rags to riches but a
small neighborhood

I turn back to the bar and the fog follows me in and the ghosts drink

And drink until the sun chases them back to the Hollywood Forever

Follow me on this journey and you will meet them all and know the truth

Or the lies we tell and the golden drunken joy that comes from the street

The ghost are alive but the real ones that breathe through pink lungs and

Eat Chinese food are waiting to talk to you and tell you their story-

come on!

A Whistling Pig

Back when beer was a crime and the
screen splashed black and white

    A whistling pig came calling for
the wizard to shine his green light

The pig became a home to Cadillacs
bearing ladies with silken hose

    Epic parties drunken and the pig
would not close

Today the pig still whistles and the par-
ties they go on

    Naked promises are given from the
starlight at dawn

A Scottish princess slings golden glasses
as she tells of castles faraway

    Contessa spins her martinis and
keeps the hounds at bay

Special K (from LA) is tired from all the
magic he performs

Carlos and Kristyn watch a Hack-
saw storm

Coleman and Curtis catch a driving beat
as the ghost girl hums

Spider monkeys are shouting and
then they turn and run

Russ and his stories unfold the history
march

While the whistling pig looks down
from the ancient wooden arch

Come one come all and sing the merry
tune

Movie stars and starlets wait for
your commune

Sara Sarah Jason Jason

Biscuit

Up at dawn she rules

2 blocks and rails

One day and dances

On another

Questions questions

Celestial questions

Swarm her air and

Cram the sidewalk

Trapped between the

Past and the present

Her life now

Is only one day

Old

Sweating shrieking

Soul dancing

Angry all-in

All-knowing

Cantankerous

Clucking conscious

Biscuit is there on

Her corner

Dancing to a

Beat only

She hears from

The Metro

Dirty sweaty

Confused

Blackened blackness

Smelly hungry

But always there

Broken hearted

Unloved untold

Unnoticed unimportant

Unhealthy

Older no wiser

Broke

But- her ruling life force goes on the appointed time each day

Biscuit oh biscuit

Twilight Stardust

Closed eyes

Red and blue lanterns

Gray green noise

Pencil yellow subway trains

Black feather marching bands

Incandescent window glass

Red horse fist bump

Mojito moon dust

Copper

Pipe

Immigrant

Spare room smash box

Piano Bar

Tucked away slyly so no one can tell

A mystical music box ringing a bell

Austin and company spray sounds in my mind

Living the piano, dancers and wine

A jewel off the boulevard, rolling the dice

Old men at the bar never think twice

Outside there is smoke, food from the grill

Inside there is whiskey and tabs climbing the hill

Music is loud we sing along

Brian on lead plays me a song

The mayor once told me the secret code

Looking out the window birds on the road

Don't go near there- you'll never come back

Good as it gets- dude that's a fact

When You're Melrose...

All day he talks

On the boulevard as they walk

Larry selling the movie stars' homes

Buy a ticket before they're all gone

But when you're Melrose- you talk to
Howard Stern

Melrose Larry Green

On the boulevard can be seen

Selling the history of our town

To all of you who are Hollywood bound

When you're Melrose you belong in the
Whack Pack

He knows the stories

Of the golden yester years

Bogey and Bacall

He makes them all appear

When you're Melrose controversy is your life

Larry's out there now

To take you on that ride

You will not forget

Melrose was your guide

Because when you're Melrose-

Hollywood is your town

Roads Made Of Red

Limos drive up

While fans get a look

Screaming and waving

"please sign my book"

All their lives

Actors work hard

Saving and scrimping

For that SAG card

But when that day comes

And they get out of bed

Knowing that now

They walk on roads made of red

Every set every scene

The lines fill their head

Hoping to see

The roads made of red

Even a hillbilly

A Clampett named Jed

Stepped into the lights

Where the roads turned red

Married to Jane

A Turner named Ted

Came to Hollywood

Where roads streaked bright red

A fairy tale land

Where reality has fled

We live in a kingdom

Where the roads are made of red

Boulevard sandwich #4

chocolate store fantasy

meters blink red

garbage truck bang

yellow blue taxi

movie stars maps

musso frank 1919

black red graffiti

one legged man

gay man smiles

happy hour specials

grocery store girl

tee shirt sale

free stress test

Meeting Kenneth Anger

I got up one morning and met

Kenneth Anger.

A Hollywood icon, Anger made scores
of avant garde films, wrote "Hollywood
Babylon", and is an authority on Aleister
Crowley.

"There he goes from the Post Office. He
crossed Wilcox with a quick gait and
sped past the Piano Bar. I blink and he
vanishes."

"Shit! I I lost him on Selma and Cahuen-
ga. I look at all 4 corners-gone!"

"before I give up I look inside Café Etc.
Bingo! He's reading the New York Times."

"I pace the side walk back and forth-
heart pounding."

"I go inside and he talks to me. Anger is warm, friendly."

"I go home. Changed."

Special K (from LA)

Hails from Colorado

    A fortunate son

King of California

    Enemy of none

Enters the Pig

    Doing the Lord's work

Never wants trouble

    Hollywood Captain Kirk

Green bottle whiskey

    Runs down his chin

Everyone knows

    He is our friend

Boulevard Sandwich #41

6600 Yucca Street

Starline Trolley #3

No Animals Allowed

No Stopping Anytime

This Property Closed

Right Turn Only

1700 Cherokee Avenue

Alexa Artiste Door

Ru Tan Weekly

Passenger Loading Only

Hollywood Community Center

Atm Fee Notice

Public Health "A"

Suits

Up and down the boulevard they stand
in windows

        Looking at foreign   tourists
and a homeless man

Sales sales sales they boast royal birth
and every color on the wheel

        Cheap cheap cheap – my God
they are cheap (at least in price)

Their neighbors are the ho clo sto's and
are clad in less (much less)

        The suits leave for much differ-
ent purposes and events

One goes to a wedding while one goes to
LAX and leaves the country

        An orange suit goes clubbing
and a purple one goes to a card game

A white one goes to a movie set and sits
in a chair for hours and hours

Come inside and buy them 3
at a time so you can wear them daily

Suits? Yep suits

Block One 6901 Greta Garbo

Dark and mysterious, the beauty of Camille

Out of shadows and onto the reel

Flesh and the devil "I vant to be alone"

Her star is silent, her fame has grown

Anna Christie the Oscar was close

I walked by and heard her ghost

Never again was one so pure

Never again was one so sure

Days of the silents, she broke the hearts

Talking in pictures Greta departs

Block Two 6819 Mabel Normand

First female screenwriter

Charlie Chaplin

Fatty Arbuckle

Murder 1922

Charles Desmond Taylor

1924 Shooting

Courtland S Dines

New York Bathing Beauty

Hal Roach Studios

Tuberculosis

Age 37

Block Three 6767 Rafael Mendez

He came from Mexico and played the coronet with Rudee Vallee

He played for Pancho Villa as a boy

Rafael is considered the best   trumpet player who ever lived

He played for the MGM Band

"perpetuum mobile"- "perpetual motion"

In the rare early morning rain I stand beside his star and feel the golden soft notes from his horn and see in the breeze the movies he played the music and made them come alive

Block Four 6743 King Vidor

King, that was his real name

Vidor, gave him the movie fame

70, that was the length of time

King, was under the Hollywood sign

Director, actor, producer and writer

King, he made the world lighter

Wizard, the Oz scenes at the start

King, his films all had heart

Hurricane, the Galveston storm

Audience, he had a brand new form

King, Vidor he can be seen

On the boulevard, he is still the King

Block Five 6685 Myrna Loy

Silent movies

Vamp

Nora Charles

The Thin Man

Helena Montana

Wales

Ocean Park

Dancing

Venice

High School

Rudolph Valentino

Cobra

Warner Brothers

Contract

Under

A Texas Moon

The

Jazz Singer

John Dillinger's

Favorite

Highest Paid

Actress

Arthur

Hornblow Jr

John

Hertz Jr

Gene

Markey, producer

Howland

H Sargeant

No children

Of her own

Spencer Tracy

Leslie Howard

Titanic Thompson

Block Six 6621 Buster Keaton

"The General is the greatest comedy, perhaps the greatest movie ever made"- Orson Welles

King of Comedy, the Great Stone Face

Houdini named him, the Buster chase

Born in vaudeville, he took the falls

World War I, hurt by the brawls

Silent movies, The Butcher Boy

Knowing Fatty, full of joy

Scores of movies, working hard

King of Comedy, quite the card

MGM, bad for Buster

Talking heads, took his luster

Now he shines, from the street

King of Comedy, still the feat!

Block Seven 6551 Basil Rathbone

To Sherlock Holmes-

Fourteen films (plus one cameo) between 1939 and 1946, Holmes came alive and told us the mysteries and how he solved them in person.

The Hound Of The Baskervilles

The Adventures Of Sherlock Holmes

Sherlock Holmes And The Voice Of Terror

The New Adventures Of Sherlock Holmes

Sherlock Holmes And The Secret Weapon

Sherlock Holmes In Washington

Sherlock Holmes Faces Death

Crazy House

The Spider Woman

The Pearl Of Death

The House Of Fear

The Woman In Green

Pursuit To Algiers

Terror By Night

Dressed To Kill

Go to his star and pay tribute to what he did for us.

Block Eight 6513 Rochester

Eddie Andersen

Gone With The Wind

Jack Benny Jack Benny

Horse Trainer Hollywood Park

Ruptured Vocal Chords

Selling Newspapers

Oakland California

Racism

Amos & Andy

Benny Death

Shock-Never The Same

Mayor Central Avenue

Fought Stereotypes

Star- Hollywood

Block Nine 6427 Gabby Hayes

Happy trails to you Gabby!

The movie star cowboy

Sidekick to Roy Rogers

Gene Autry

Wild Bill Elliott

John Wayne

Randolph Scott

North Hollywood Apartments

Manager

National Cowboy & Western Heritage Museum

Blazing Saddles

Happy trails to you Gabby!

Block Ten 6363
William S Hart

Hart was a cowboy on the silent
screen

Friends with Wyatt back in
'eighteen

Courageous and honest, that was
his code

Owned Billy's pistols and
villains he mowed

Born in New York, Shakespeare he
mastered

Meant for the saddle, never a
bastard

He knew Bat Masterson, and doz-
ens of heroes

The Indians attacked him
with all their arrows

Tom Mix, Roy Rogers, and the Lone
Ranger

     All tipped their hats to the cowboy
avenger

One of the first to get his own star

     I tip my own hat to William S Hart

Cloudy day Sunny week

Cloudy day a sunny week

The boulevard is the same

Cloudy day a sunny week

I am always changing

Sunny day a sunny week

Old shoes in the morning

Sunny day a sunny week

Girls crying in their coffee

Jazzy day a mellow week

Old man in the garbage can

Jazzy day a sunny week

Fog is rolling in faster

Hollywood days and Hollywood nights

Beer is getting hot

Hollywood days and Hollywood nights

The street lights are broken

Policeman's Viewpoint

Black and white coming right at me

I swear it wasn't me

Blue man with his hand cuffs

He knows it wasn't me

Rules and rules falling on my head

The ride downtown was rough

Headaches and love drunk

He smiles and says "that's tough"

Policeman with a viewpoint

More dangerous than bombs

Back on the boulevard

Looking at the palms

The Mayor (Don Porter)

He is my brother and true to his be-
liefs that have brought him down a
rocky road but now the journey is bet-
ter-smoother.

He was there from the first and befriend-
ed me to the core like few ever have and I
miss him and his heart-soul.

Born on the same day but a different
year he believed in me and my words but
there were things he needed and I un-
derstand-really.

He is still The Mayor and brother let me
tell you there can be only one because
the town's not big enough for more-or
less.

He was king of the castle and knew every
lock and unlock in his domain because
he earned the right-wrong.

The Mayor still lives and man I am glad
because without him we would all perish
and go down a wrong path-road.

Whenever you see him please tip your hat and tell him you remember how he is and always will be - The Mayor

Beat Love

Something's right something's wrong

Living in the beat the soul belongs

Without love the boat breaks in two

Without love the hole becomes the shoe

On the beat turtles run fast

Pigeons fly higher as they soar past

The fog parts and the pirates come
ashore

Without love the tears die on the floor

Something's right something's wrong

Hear the troubadour strumming his song

Gather love and let the heart burst open

Everyone know how hard they are coping

Failure heartbreak lies and trouble

Cannot break the beat love bubble

Hear me now and hear me later

Beat love keeps the path much straighter

Traffic Hum-roar

The machinery never stops it flows burps honks

Organ grinder locust honey stains the street

Jazz beaumonts fly hard at you smash the wall

Cars cars cars jettison their crappy flea bag from the glass

Noise oh god the noise the sound of electric knives cutting

Peace peace peace early morning peace smells

Day light hours have the bee keepers busy smoking

Bells bells bells ring for the horses to feed up

Guards roll past waving flags of despair

Words words words to sell the shelves of

nothingness

Beer whiskey wine gin sour grapes and no money

Paper dreams in the dark hammers into wet pulp

Fiction non fiction shorts pants blue cameras and fries

Hot dogs burgers go in and out until they grow dark

Help no help money from above and be-low

Raging fever pitch music that dulls skulls

Target play tag across the black pave-ment cross walk

Buses buses big buses stop go halt sneer

Day after day machinery never stops

Burps farts honks screeches pop explode dies

He Still Asks Me Why?

The brown man stands in front of his little tee shirt store and grins and nods at me every day I walk past on my way to the Post Office. Sometimes I stop and buy some new shirts and talk to him.

Born in Viet Nam but he is old now. His is wife is long dead. His children, and he had six are long dead. His brothers and sisters are long dead. Most of his friends are long dead.

None died from old age. They were all killed. Some from rockets. Some from bullets. Some from grenades. Some were blown to bits by bombs. There are no graves to visit some because there were no bodies left.

The common thread to all their deaths is they were all killed by Americans. He was not a Communist. He still grieves. He only asks me questions because I am old enough to know about all this. He thinks I should be able to tell him the answer. He only asks me why?

Why did Americans come and invade his country and kill his entire family? He

would still grieve if he knew the answer. He thinks I owe him that. I hang my head and shame and have no answer except America loves war. Always have.

Well Whiskey

Often when the light fades

And the city noise dims into the gutters

I drift into a certain lullaby conscious-
ness

And the saloon doors swing open

The fly buzzes and lands

The seat opens up and the turmoil be-
gins

What do I want? She asks

I don't have to think

Or contemplate much

I yell out "well whiskey"

Well whiskey is, well, it comes from the
well

She brings it to me in a dwarf's cup

I like to look at it sitting on the old wooden bar

The sun glimmers and a laser of golden
light

Pierces the liquid and stabs my eye

I launch it past my lips and feel the hot

Stream of oafish water hit my   stomach
nerves

And shake my soul and then my extrem-
ities

Well whiskey, well it comes from the well

I see my eye sight is now better and my
voice

Is louder but never too loud

Maybe my ears are more sensitive

The dwarf glass is empty and I   contem-
plate

Its role in this wonderful place

Well whiskey, well it flows from the well

Expecting Apple Boxes

Long ago when the road was calling me
back to a monk's journey-

A wild oat epiphany on a cold fall after-
noon-

Golden burnt red sun stirred a knife
sharp wind-

Apple boxes, empty apple boxes were
cast aside-

My mind's eye yelled me over from the
tavern-

Standing in a little wind vector from the
sky-

The apple boxes began to lift, swirl, and
turn-

My life swirled inside the cardboard tor-
nado-

Speaking words that cannot be   spoken-

Pleading me to stay and not to get on

that road-

My heart exploded, melted, but later
became hard-

Now I feel a different call-

I long to stand in that wild oat corner-

I want to see that golden burnt red sun-

I want to see those apple boxes swirl-

I expect that old wind will soon return-

Where the Dinosaurs Roam

Once they were famous

If only for a while

Now they are older

Their telephones have a dial

Black and white made them

Look young and strong

Up in the hills

They still sing their song

Cars in the drive

Ancient but new

Gloves on the wheel

Now they are few

The bygone era

Has trapped them there

Movies re-mastered

Forever to share

Kissing and swooning

Not naked or crude

Men with fedoras

Smoky attitude

Their lives still run

And they go on

Older and forgotten

Blankets they don

Saw her yesterday

Behind shades of black

She smiled and nodded

Waited for my attack

I bowed and left her

Not a word could I say

Living in the past

Longing for yesterday

Notes to a fool

She thinks she is wonderful

Talking so loud

Center of attention

Just a giant black hole

Judgmental

Never her fault

Someone else to blame

Volcano of madness

Looking to fight

Veteran of wars

Always claiming victory

Hides behind the white flag

Straight shooter

Aims for the heart

Crying in the dark

For friends or anybody

A fool who

Believes her own rules

Rules

That built her a jail of silence

Humble yourself!

Look around

Life and people are wonderful

Give love

Not money

Money

You love so dear

Making you lonely

Smile

Listen

Care

With your heart

Not with your words

Come back!

To the world

Before it doesn't ever want you again

Carmel Traces

sweet foam

lips of red

broken heart

low cut blouse

boards metro train

legs so long

window glaze

doesn't talk

sees my stare

grimaces 'go away'

can't help myself

she gets off

I blink as she

spills the cup

gone

all is left

are

carmel traces

Carpe Noctrum

Ah, when that old magic sun

Creeps back into his coffin

Ah, the signal is felt deep

In the loins of those still alive

Ah, a voice is broadcast

"come out and play"

Girls with tiny dresses

And giraffe shoes

Boys with pills

Who prey on the awkward

Old men now dead

And have one vein beating

Old women laugh, curse

At the absurdity

All night clerks

With shot guns and fear

Hot doggers slap

Mustard and fried onions

They all outlast

Deep sleepers at home

Bodies deaf to the night

Ignoring the sirens

Ticket takers

At old movie houses

Live for a failed

Box office fable

Subway train drivers

Watch pukers as the

Light shines into

Tunnels of dark wonder

All night coffee shoppers

Who bite on stale bread

And accept a caffeine surge

Rub their tired backs

And grab at the dark night

Twisting and shucking it

Like corn and eat

Raw kernels

Corn juice runs madly

Down the chins

And suddenly, slowly

It's over, done

Dark Corners

Look lure stare scan apple access

Virtuous vine bull belch wanton western

Frank fools colored concoction   tasted
tricks

Moans multitude organs occur weeds
wilted

Naked nature wordy welcome hearty
hellion

Juted jackboot pillow pig jazz   jumble

Song solution pizza proud shot solid

Lowdown cheese children melted motive

Bare ballerina shaved sidetrack blonde
banker

Endless ending

The lowly "I"

Flushing all worldly

Desire from the body

And searing the flesh

With the truth you

Can get down to the "I",

The true self, the lowly

"I"

When the road

Gets long and the

Body needs a drink

Or rest or comfort

And you can never

Find enough

You can get down

To the lowly "I"

On the rugged streets

Of Hollywood, or Paris

Or a little town

In Texas, and the man

With the brass horn

Comes, you get

To the "I"

The true "I"

The lowly "I"

Someday when

You are alone

And watch some

Mindless TV show

A bird flies by

The window

You look at him

As he returns

And lock eyes

To see the "I"

The real "I"

In the lowest

Hour your tears

Flow like clear

Blood and you

Hunger for ice cream

But have no money

You stare in the mirror

You begin

To see the

"I"

When the door

Is locked

Your keys lie

At the bottom

Of a sewer drain

No one hears

Your cries

Your voice calls

Out for that

Singular "I"

Sometimes that "I"

Saves the day

And shows you

All your molecules

From the past

And turns and

Gives you a glimpse

Of the gypsy

The "I" smiles

And disappears

Like smoke

Puzzles and Circles

Hollywood and Wilcox trying to   under-
stand

Dark clouds and tour buses raining their
brand

Siamese twins barking like seals for a
dollar

Wrinkled old man down in the squalor

Sirens go by as hustlers sling dirty words

Hollywood's a poem crazy and   absurd

Up and down the street blows a golden
peace

Up and down the hills roams the filthy
beast

Sidewalk café changing her name

Fingers on the keyboards playing the
game

Puzzles and circles brand new paint

Cops on horseback worshipping a saint

Puzzles and circles Hollywood fear

Tourists with money wasted on beer

Puzzles and circles sun going down

DJ's spinning same old sound

Heart strings from a Bull-frog

Demons hiss and rise from a heavy man hole cover at

Midnight to inhabit oily black alleys and prey on the foolish

Flying and swooping down from the old building tops

Sea gulls full grown flap away hard as they feel the black night coming

The ghost, the chief, he is ready to emerge from the

Griffith woods with his latest conquest to show the lesser ghosts

In his paw are bloody strings that are a

mystery

Defiled and disgusting they are frail and
quake

Heart strings from a bullfrog or some-
thing I can not tell

But there is no doubt the previous owner
is now dead and gone

Chief must have bartered for such a
dark hard to find

Item in the weekly trade markets under-
ground

Heart strings from a bull frog what a sto-
ry they tell

From drunken radios that float down the
obsidian river

Frogland the kingdom of pleasure and

knowledge

Frogland where bulls and lady frogs
dance the frog love

Heart strings that are guarded by holy
relics and blood rituals

Not even witches and warlocks dare pos-
sess

But Chief and his devious ways now
wear them necklace style

Making them beat his chest like a para-
mount drum

Heart strings from a bullfrog now stain
boulevard

All who come near fee their own life
shortened

Shutting Down (the street)

Gasps of joy

    Curses of defeat

Burly black suits

    Grab metal fences

Roll out the red

    Keep it clean

People gape and line up

    Others spit in disgust

Tourists from outer hell

    Block everything

Impossible black cars

    Crowd to unload

There they are!

    Cries, shouts, screams

A lonely bar man stumbles out

      Who? What? Crap

Bread on ancient tables

      Watch them depart

Junkies with a sweet ache

      Mutter curses

The cars leave

      The fences fold up

The street re-opens

Black Star Licorice
Lincoln Star

Daybreak comes with a thud sounding
the alarm

Or maybe just a heralding   trumpet
announcing the arrival

Big black licorice Lincoln star pants
cinched low

Street swagger sweats and cars cruise
calling cash

Big black Lincoln star digs in the trash
can

Sun beats noon hour tour buses ev-
erywhere

Universal cry for money or pot or help

Big black Lincoln star dances across
Orange

Sneaks into the Roosevelt and pisses in

the nice toilet

Night moons shine down jazzy
sounds sway

Boulevard breeze blows backwards Scoo-
by sells succulent sizzle

Big black licorice Lincoln star seeks
somewhere silent sleep

In-and-Out

The sign calls me down to Sunset and
the smell pushes me through the door

I think of The Dude while I order and the
hard labor he might deplore

Animal style and nowhere to sit among
the crowds who crave the same

I should have said "to go" as my   energy
drains fast

My number is called and I carry it out
beside a palm tree

Delicious beyond belief I feel my blood
rush as my bladder calls

Watching the night Sunset traffic my
mood is Leopard strong

The passing car's radio plays a country
song

I head up Orange and into the hotel's
ultra-clean restrooms

Hot water forces a yowl and I wipe
my red hands on cotton towels

In-and-Out is the night tonic for this
strange life

In-and-Out washes away troubles,
demons, strife, and even hunger

Cloud Candy in a Western Sky

She looks down

   A medieval princess

Begs me for a look

   A climb

Her forlorn face

   Strikes my soul

In the distance

   Windy pillars fall

She is gone

   My love, my soul

I name her Medusa

   And her castle Blunderbus

She is held there

   Songs of misery play

My poor broken heart

   It sobs

I am inconsolable

   Unable to reach Blunderbus

Then on a summer day

   I see her, clear, large, smiling

I launch myself upward

   Flying higher

I wrap my arms around her

   And then disappear

Red Line Blues

Life's full of trouble and the day has been hell

Coming down stairs three women fell

Blues were playing the beat was fine

Not finding a seat on the late   arriving Red Line

The train jerks hard and now we're off

Sick old man hacking his cough

Thoughts do ramble must change my ways

New resolutions from the dark train maze

We are together riding down the track

Singing the blues and man there's a stack

Blue lights flash and Seventh's ahead

Beggar climbs in asking for bread

Union's next and we all depart

Ending better than the Red Line start

Kool Kafe Breeze Monkeys

Late late at night when the bedroom
lights are dark and the beast   coppers
are looking for someone to bust

The kool kafe breeze monkeys are safe
inside where the beer and smoke glisten
the brick walls coating the music

Outside a man cries a southern bible
chant about the wandering worlds of
crazy pools

Inside they watch disgraced doctors
undergoing a medieval bloodletting while
one of them shouts "someone's cheat-
ing!"

The breeze monkeys laugh at suits so
square they can't roll on the little dance
floor

The chef whips up a batch of fresh whis-
key soup for the horse who is so frost
bitten he drools

The breeze monkeys sit above the fray

and look down at the wooden jump ap-
ples

White napkin cavalry troops order rum
until the glasses fade into a red cow
milk shake

A pot head politician throws   comedy
jokes on a gin mill   prostitute wear-
ing grandma's thong

A high roller strolls in with his light
house gamble shoes and suddenly the
dull knife pirate crowd shoots and kills
him

A waitress pushes the nurse's snack
wagon causing the monkeys to act out
shaved head moron gestures

One monkey looks up Janis Joplin's
skirt and steals a little girl's back pack
to use later for future ladder crimes

The lace curtain gypsies battle the axe
murderer's kitten making the usual sus-
pects offer up confessions

Their oil driven motives shatter when
confronted with alphabet crowned head

stubble mats

Now the pony express cleavage is ex-
posed and the thunder head panties
drop to the floor shocking the crack head
bankers

And what do the kool kafe breeze mon-
keys see? YOU!

Razzle Dazzle Man

Night falls softly on the street corner
blues

The razzle dazzle man sits on his stool to
play

With his coffee colored skin

And his thread bare suit

And his dusty hat

And his drift wood guitar

And his polished two toned shoes

And his buck toothed smile

Melodies of a broken heart

Stories pour out as the all night girls
walk by

They drop quarters and giggle

Upstairs the broken glass hears

Songs from the past

Songs by the whiskey faced men

Songs from the pirate ship wars

Inside the guitar a cannon explodes

Now a black cat insomniac paws to see

The razzle dazzle man going home

The Great California Earthquake of 2014

In the early darkness peace when Holly-
wood's in the last stages of the same old
dream sleep of hope and despair

And the homeless are still shivering up
last week's LA Times

It came calling

Hell's jack hammer shook the tall build-
ings into jelly spined jitterbugs dancing
the Charleston

Silently, then with a crash, it found me

Bed slats sounding like a Louisville slug-
ger on Tom Sawyer's fence

The invisible wrecking ball shook me
hard

My bed became a race horse with the
"up" and "down" of the turn down the
home stretch

It stopped

Then it rolled sideways

Trapped in the sheets I rolled

A human rolling pin the floor stopped

My imagined descent in to the hard
parking lot

Two floors below

It was over

(for now)

Days later it came back

Joined by its twin brother

Andy Dick

Just Josh and me

Rather Josh and I

Yearned for a quick beer

And that's all

To talk

Of things

Demons

Dragons

Heroes

Villains

The Pig and Whistle

Didn't mind

One half beer later

Andy and friend strolled by

Josh knew what to do

My head spun twice

Andy took the stool

Next to mine

Long lost brother

Although the prodigal

He took the liberty of visiting

Our souls

By the 2nd round

We were all

Pals, comrades, confidants,patrons,
backers, self- creators

We told stories

Sang songs

We laughed

Leaving, I apologized

Josh carried on

Andy was happy

Boulevard Marine Layer Cake

Cold and heavy

Gray wet loneliness

Blankets the low sky

Silver buffalo herds of ocean magic

Spread their dull ghost hooves

Across the willing sky

The boulevard's cake bakes in a chilly oven:

Spoon sauce candy

Ancient thought squares

Marble top misery

Short skirt paper

Disappearing autos

Yellow fog eyes

Green man (and bicycle)

Pizza window glow

Street sweeper howl

Key locks of hope

Tiny ball of sunshine

BUFFALO HERD RETREATS

Little darling, little darling

Too late, too late

The cake is all gone

STOLEN

Stress Test Pigeons

On a sunny rooftop morn

Where Pigeon Town moved overnight

Marvin(the pigeon) said to Pantsuit Allie(another pigeon)

M: O where is Gertrude? Where has she gone?

PSA: She was stressed out honey, very stressed.

M: I know Allie, but where O where did she go?

PSA: Down there to the Seedology Blue and Whites.

M: O God! O no!

PSA: It's ok honey, they tested her. It's ok.

M: No, it can't be ok, it's bad, very bad.

PSA: Honey, Gertrude was stressed out.

M: You know they will clip off some of her feathers, don't you? She will fly lop sided.

PSA: Seedology says some of have too many feathers. They weigh us down when it rains.

M: It never rains.

PSA: O.

Flowers On Sunday

Hollywood Sundays are peerless when the streets are blocked off

When the wagons pull in with their flowers and corn and honey and beans and squash and breakfast and banjos and coffee

Folks walk the dogs and kids and lean into the canopies of jewels, of piles of oranges, of hot food cooking, and rows of lemons and limes and mangoes and cucumbers

Buckets of flowers sit in cold water preaching hope, beauty, and majesty

So simple

So beautiful

When Hollywood has flowers on Sunday

Pink Hudson

Pink Hudson Pink Hudson

A favored few enter your gates

Pink Hudson Pink Hudson

A Moroccan villa's legend awaits

Pink Hudson Pink Hudson

I dream of your ghosts, magic, and charm

Pink Hudson Pink Hudson

You create enough stories to buy the farm

The ghosts call me to enter their past

Goldwyn and Valentino ask me to outlast

Chaplin sings his song to a woman I once knew

Pink Hudson Pink Hudson

I need to come home and live with you

Hit & Run Harry

Hit & Run Harry was born in Japan

He came to America and got
California plates

His 4 black wheels are now the
terror of Hollywood

And beyond

Why?

He loves to hit people!

Harry dwells in a dirty little
Hollywood garage

Turn him loose!

Over the years he has run over old
people and children

And a lot of just ordinary folks

Fueled by unleaded gas and coffee

He runs over people in Santa

Monica

And Wilshire

And Victory

And 6th Street

And Downey

Harry has to hurry home because he almost got caught

He gets away and laughs

And laughs and laughs

Street Guitar Prophets

Sleeping in the park their funds are
quite low

Playing for the masses the prophets
shine the show

Some are always bad and others play so
good

Old guitars without cases, scars deep in
the wood

The prophets look hungry, their songs
are the key

Unlock the dollar menu and moment to
feel free

Down on their luck and a heart full of
sorrow

Empty pocket syndrome nothing they
can borrow

The songs are a bundle of old rock and
blues

Their clothes are frightful with holes in
their shoes

Working days of 7 and smoking weed
they found

Squeezing strings of memory with a dull
and crappy sound

They break my heart with tunes of pover-
ty row

Then they glue it together when they
start another show

Basket of Bricks

Dark alley night

Drunk and alone

Pondering soul misery

Stumbling home

Old buildings tower

Layers of paint

Gargoyles of mystery

Never a saint

Brick after brick

Cracks up the wall

Leaning against them

Knees buckle and fall

Dark alley night

Drunk and alone

Staring upward

Maybe a broken bone

Hearing a racket

Devoid of a light

Stomach is churning

Windy cold night

The rackets gets louder

Guessing it's a magic trick

My head is pounding

Like a basket of bricks

6438 Cantinflas

Born Mario Alfonso Moreno Reyes in Mexico

Made millions laugh

Even Chaplin

"He was the greatest!"

6 of 12 children

Catinflas was his beloved character who was:

Beloved

Reviled

Examined

Enjoyed

Helped usher in the golden age of cinema

To Mexico

David Niven

Around the world in 80 days

Cantinflas was a star!

6426 Clyde McCoy

For seventy years Clyde played jazz

Played the trumpet but inspired the Wah-Wah pedal

Wah-wah went his trumpet

Cry Baby sounds

Sugar Blues

Hits in the 1930's

Billboard Magazine

Johnny Mercer

"Have you heard these blues

That I'm goin' to sing to you?

When you hear them

They will thrill you through and through

They're the sweetest blues you ever heard

Now listen and don't say a word

Sugar Blues, everybody singin'

The Sugar Blues, the whole town's ringin'

My lovin' man sweet as he can be

But the dog gone fool turned sour on me!

6412 Tex Williams

Sollie Paul Williams hailed from Ramsey, Illinois

His Western Caravan recorded polkas for Capitol Records

But all that changed when Tex sang "Smoke, Smoke, Smoke"

"Now I'm a fella with a heart of gold

And the ways of a gentleman I've been told

The kind of guy who wouldn't harm a flea

But if me and a certain character met

The guy who invented the cigarette

I'd murder that son-of-a gun in the first degree

Smoke, smoke, smoke that cigarette

Puff, puff, puff and if you smoke yourself

to death

Tell St Peter at the Golden Gate

That you hate to make him wait

But you got to have another
cigarette

6356 Queen

Celebrate!

Freddie, Brian, John and Roger

Celebrate!

Smile

Sheer Heart Attack

A Night At The Opera

Bohemian Rhapsody

18 Million Number Ones

300 Million Sold

Rock and Roll Hall of Fame 2001

Good bye Freddie

Hollywood bows to all of you

Celebrate!

6320 Tab Hunter

Arthur Gelien of German parents

Who divorced and his mother

Moved to California

His good looks made the change

Tab

Tab Hunter

40 movies

Island of Desire

Battle Cry

Natalie Wood

Sophia Loren

Debbie Reynolds

The Burning Hills

Young Love

Ninety-Nine Ways

The Tab Hunter Show

The boy next door

The sweet heart

The marine

The cowboy

6312 King Baggot

"The King Of The Movies"

Actor Director Screenwriter

The Most Photographed Man In The World

The man whose face is as familiar as the man in the moon

269 Movies

Wrote 18 screen plays

Directed 45

The Scarlet Letter

Ivanhoe

Dr Jekyll and Mr Hyde

Tumbleweeds

Lived in Venice

Died and buried in Los Angeles

Who were you?

Why don't we know?

1645 Vine Delores Costello

The Goddess of the Silent Screen

Born in Pittsburgh

Parents trod the boards

Child actress

Vitagraph Films

1909 A Midsummer Night's dream

Sea Beast

Warner Brothers

The Goddess of the Silver Screen

Grandmother of Drew Barrymore

Her spirit lives in heart of Hollywood

63 Movies 63

Let's raise a glass to Delores!

1623 Vine Edna May Oliver

Edna Edna!

You quit school at 14

You knew that the stage the screen
would be your life

Edna Edna!

Broadway and Bogart soon called your
name

Then Hollywood and the movie roles
beckoned

Edna Edna!

Tart tongued spinster

Wizard came a calling but it was not to
be

But many more called

Wife in Name only

Three O'Clock in the Morning

Restless Wives

Icebound

Manhattan

The Lady Who Lied

The Lucky Devil

48 in all

Tip your hats to Edna!

1617 Vine Adolph Zukor

Born in Hungary

Came to America

Promised a girl he would bring her over

Lived with parents

Toiled in an upholstery shop

Apprenticed to a furrier

The girl came too late

Never spoke again

19 years old

Designed and sold his own fur line

Zukor's Novelty Fur Company

25 employees

Built a house on 300 acres

Pool golf course

Bought hundreds more acres

And then and then

Created Paramount Pictures

www.ingramcontent.com/pod-product-compliance
Lightning Source LLC
Chambersburg PA
CBHW070809050426
42452CB00011B/1960